CATS & KITTENS

AT HOME AND IN THE WILD

With an introduction by Adriano Torregrossa

CRESCENT BOOKS

Contents

- 3 Foreword
- 5 The great family of felines
- 6 The wild cat: breeds and sub-divisions
- 7 The origins of the domestic cat
- 9 Domestic cats
  Persian cats
- 10 Siamese cats
  Blue cats
  Tailless cats
- 11 Habits and character
- 13 Rearing your cat
- 14 Distribution of the principal members of the cat family
- 15 Principal breeds of domestic cat

Acknowledgments are due to the following for photographs used in this volume:

Bavaria-Lüty: 2, 13, 27, 94
Carlo Bevilacqua: 90
Bruce Coleman Ltd: 100, 102, 103
C. Dani: 4, 9, 14, 20, 25, 26, 31, 33, 37–41, 51–57, 59–63, 67, 68, 70, 71, 74–79, 81, 83, 84, 86, 88, 89, 91, 92, 93, 95, 96
Edistudio: page 5
EPS: 11, 15, 19, 23, 49
Elettra Cliché: 106
Farabola: 64
Hamlyn Picture Library: page 4
Intercamera: 6, 7, 8, 10, 12, 72, 85
Istituto Geografico De Agostini: 97
D. Margiocco: 104
Mercurio: 105
M. Orfini: 18, 28–30, 32, 34, 36, 42–48, 50, 65, 66, 69, 73, 82, 87
L. Pellegrini: 101
P. Popper: 35
Radio Times Picture Library: page 8
Tierbilder Okapia: 17, 21, 22
G. Tomsich: 99
Transworld: 1, 16, 24
ZFA: 58, 80

Translated from the Italian of Adriano Torregrossa

© Istituto Geografico De Agostini, Novara 1967
English edition © Orbis Publishing Limited, London 1972
Revised edition 1973
Printed in Italy by IGDA, Novara
Library of Congress Catalog Card No: 76-188866

It is always difficult to write a relatively short work on a subject like cats without becoming too superficial. It is such a vast, well-explored subject and, to add to the writer's difficulties, one which presents such varied and familiar aspects.

In fact, we were faced with several possible alternatives. On the one hand, we could have decided on an educational approach based strictly on the scientific data, but this would not have been written in the easy, agreeable style which the reader of a book like this has a right to expect. On the other hand, we could have abandoned the technical terms and descriptions and limited ourselves to accompanying the very handsome photographs which illustrate this book with trite captions and a chatty commentary. Both alternatives represent extremes of simplification.

We have therefore found a compromise: the text is at once instructive and agreeable; it is easy to read and understand while at the same time the information is accurate and up to date. In short, we have tried to supply interesting information about the life of the cat, its character, its reasonable demands on us, its place in the vast world of nature and the homes of man, together with practical suggestions for looking after it, while taking care not to be pedantic or boring.

That is why we have divided the text into a number of sections, each illustrating a different aspect of our study. We felt this would make it easier for the reader to refer back to the information or to isolate details which particularly interest him.

The first sections are short. They are only intended to describe the cat's place in the great family of felines, and to narrate some of the legends surrounding its origin, side by side with some of the known facts.

The sections which follow are longer and fuller since they concern the cat as we know it and its place in our lives, but also because we wanted to present the domestic cat as the hero of this book.

We have also included some important observations on the rearing and feeding of cats. We hope they will be useful to the reader. We have tried to keep the whole account simple and compelling so that it would seem more like an informal conversation between animal lovers about a creature which is eminently worth regarding as our friend.

Adriano Torregrossa

Opposite: The cat's uncanny knack for landing on its feet is proverbial. Below: The teeth structure of carnivores has altered comparatively little since prehistoric times. The Miacidae, which became extinct approximately 40 million years ago, had 44 teeth (incisors, canines, premolars and molars). The Canidae have lost two upper molars; the Felidae have been reduced to 30 teeth; the Otariidae have evolved with teeth especially suited to catching fish.

The great family of felines

As everyone knows, the cat is a mammal, a member of that great animal family, the felines, which is without any doubt one of the most admired, respected and feared families in the world. It contains a remarkable variety of individual types which zoologists have classified into different groups according to certain common characteristics.

Conspicuous among these basic characteristics are the retractile claws, protected by the end of the paw when the animal is in movement, or unsheathed when needed; the whiskers, which are endowed with extreme tactile sensitivity; and the special structure of the pupil, vertically elongated and capable of considerable dilation depending on the brightness of the cat's surroundings.

All felines are carnivores and predators, at least in their original state. Even the domestic cat retains this instinct. It has become almost omnivorous as a result of its association with man, sharing his way of life and his diet, but the mere sight of a mouse will suddenly reawaken all the instincts inherent in its nature. Also there are cats which, inoffensive when young, develop into crafty, skilful thieves when they grow older, ready to threaten such other domestic pets as canaries or goldfish.

Moreover, this is just as true for the great felines which have been raised in the circus or zoo. They seem as gentle as lambs until the very moment when, their instincts suddenly roused, they launch themselves at the nearest prey.

The cat is not the only feline which can be domesticated. There is also the cheetah, which is the oddest of all cats and is a sort of intermediary between the dog family and the cat family. It lacks retractile claws, it is a faster runner than other felines, it is less agile when climbing. Once it has been domesticated, it is faithful, obedient, and affectionate towards its master so, by its nature if not by its appearance, resembling the dog rather than the cat.

Contrary to popular belief, those felines which at first sight most resemble the domestic cat, such as the wild cat

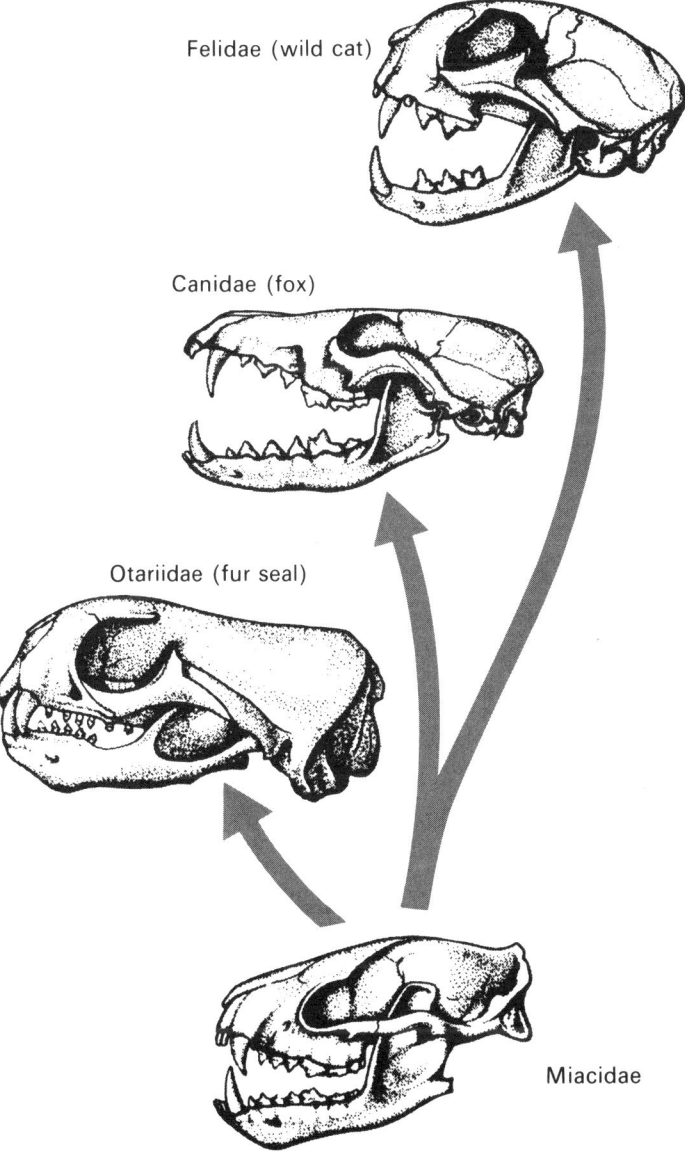

Felidae (wild cat)

Canidae (fox)

Otariidae (fur seal)

Miacidae

The African wild cat, *Felis Lybica*, is probably the ancestor of the domestic cat. Here you can see its position in the animal kingdom traced through the classifications of genus, family, order, class and phylum.

and the lynx, can only be domesticated with great effort and infinite patience. Attempts to tame some particularly recalcitrant specimens prove fruitless.

In captivity certain members of the cat family breed with difficulty. The cheetah had never been bred in captivity until 1956, in Philadelphia Zoo in the United States, but the three cubs died of feline distemper. The first successful upbringing was in 1960 at Krefeld Zoo in Germany. A few more cheetahs have been bred since then, in zoos in England and Italy as well, but a litter of cheetahs is still a notable event. Tigers and jaguars also breed with difficulty in zoos.

In limiting this account to those felines which belong to the same group as the cat (genus *Felis*), mention must be made, apart from the common wild cat – and excluding the lynx, which belongs to its own genus, *Lynx* – of the serval, whose muzzle and skin are very like those of the cheetah but which is much smaller in size. Like the cheetah, the serval is easy to tame and has a gentle, affectionate nature.

Also included are those felines which for one reason or another present certain similarities to the domestic cat; but this book is devoted to the best-known felines, which the poet has described as 'strong and gentle, the pride of the household'.

The wild cat

There is a fairly widespread belief, which is without any foundation, that the domestic cat is descended from the European wild cat. In fact, this feline, which is found in Europe (where it is facing extinction), Asia, Africa and America, belongs to the same genus as the domestic cat, but the two species differ considerably. In addition, there are a number of different species of wild cat throughout the world.

The European wild cat displays certain characteristics which are peculiar to itself and which exclude the possibility of close kinship with the domestic cat. Its body is more heavily built, its limbs longer and its tail a much more important feature. The fur, which is yellowish and very thick on the tail, has black markings. Its extremities, like its ears, are black.

Apart from the European wild cat, authorities recognise a number of other species of small feline which live in a wild state throughout the continents.

In Asia, the classification of species shows certain clear differences. The *jungle cat* or *Chaus* can be regarded as an animal which is between the lynx and the wild cat. Its general appearance resembles that of the lynx but its nature is calmer and more easygoing, and it possesses certain different bodily characteristics. The *Pallas cat* or *Manul*, which is found mostly in the steppes of Central Asia, has a body less heavy than that of the wild cat. It is a very dangerous creature, courageous and aggressive. The *fishing cat* or *viverrine* lives mainly in India. Its diet consists almost exclusively of fish which it catches with extraordinary dexterity; it does not hesitate to venture into the village where it constitutes a threat to all domestic animals.

The wild cat most commonly found in Asia as well as in Africa, however, is the African wild cat or bush cat (*Felis lybica*). The Nubian wild cat is a sub-species of the African wild cat. It is most frequently found in Nubia; in build and general appearance it is very similar to the domestic cat, although the colour of its fur is quite different. It is to this cat that most naturalists trace the origins of the domestic cat. Today it appears certain that this animal was first domesticated by the Egyptians and that all the breeds and sub-species of the domestic cat itself can be considered to be its descendants.

The considerable differences between the different species cannot be regarded as an argument against this thesis. It is not possible to retrace the evolutionary development of the cat with the necessary accuracy. Even to this day it is difficult to choose animals from which to breed a well-defined species, because of the peculiarly feline practice of indiscriminate mating among the different races. Therefore we are forced to limit our study to rather scant and superficial characteristic similarities.

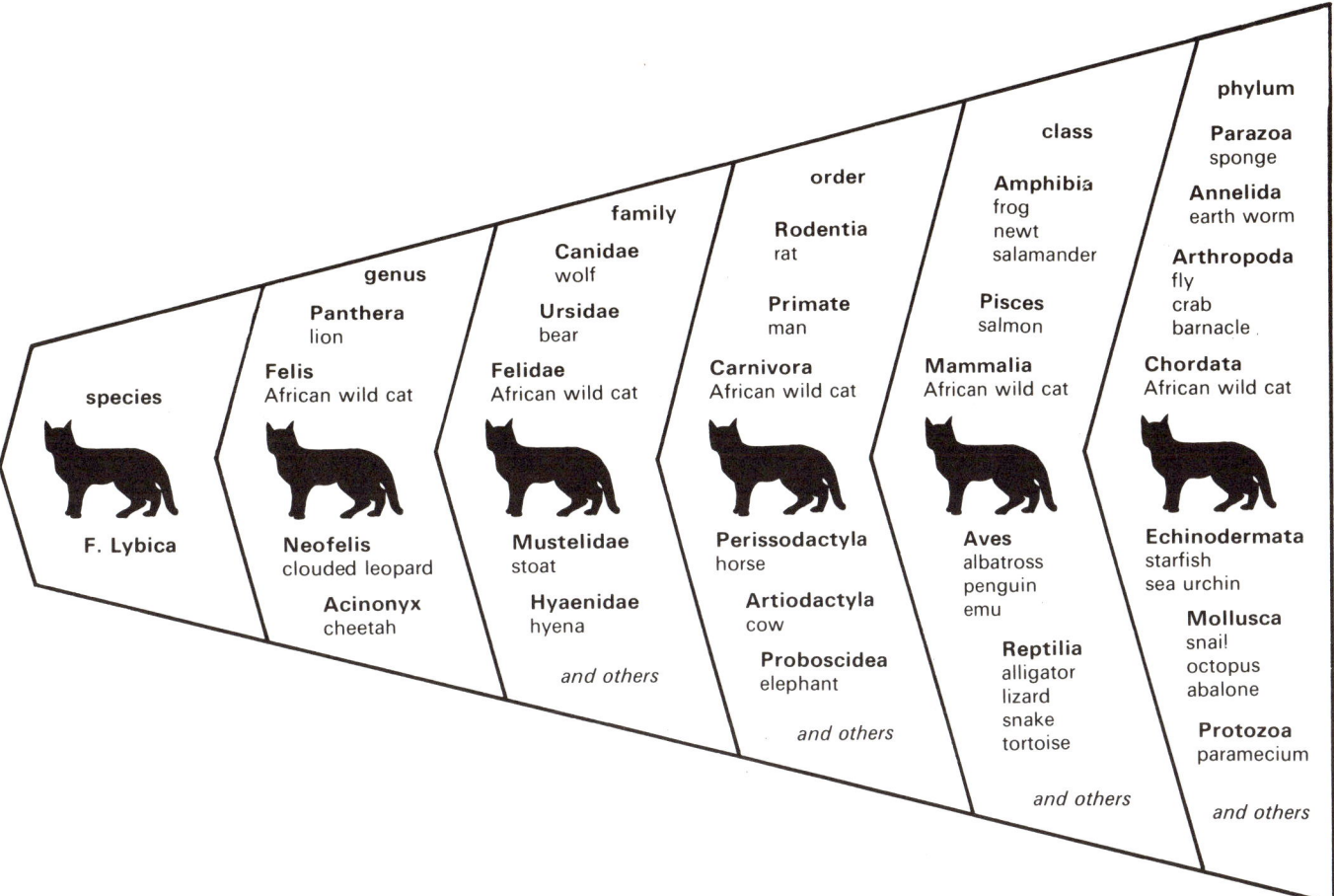

Taking these circumstances into account, it must be admitted that numerous factors tend to indicate that the Nubian wild cat is the most likely ancestor of the domestic cat.

Origins of the domestic cat

According to a Greek legend, the goddess Diana created the cat in order to ridicule the lion, which had been created by her brother Apollo.

Another legend, this time of Muslim origin, describes the cat as being born of the insane passion – reciprocated – of a monkey for a superb lioness.

Hebrew folklore also contains a charming legend to explain the cat's origin. It seems that domestic cats did not exist before the Flood. Aboard the Ark, among the survivors from the flooded world, were some rats who consumed the survivors' provisions. In desperation Noah begged the Lord to send him the means to fight this scourge. The Lord sent him a completely unexpected remedy: the lion sneezed and out of the sneeze came a pretty little cat.

These ancient theories about the cat's origin are not devoid of a certain poetry, but they are scarcely probable. It is much more likely that this animal has been in existence from very distant ages; the cat's remote origins can be assessed from fossil remains up to 50 million years old which give evidence of its parentage together with that of other felines and even, at least in the earliest eras, animals including the family of dogs, weasels and seals.

It would be too ambitious to attempt a description here, however approximate, of the cat's genetic evolution and the differences which have been established between the actual species and their original stock. It would also take too long to examine the evolution of each individual species. This study, therefore, must limit itself to remembering that the fossil remains of cats go back to the earliest neolithic period of the Stone Age; therefore it can be seen that its origins as a clearly distinguished animal are by no means recent.

As previously mentioned, the first domesticated cat was probably a Nubian wild cat, *Felis lybica*. The first documents we have relating to the history of its domestication are Egyptian, and date from 1668 BC. The Ancient Egyptians had already succeeded in 'improving' the feline race and there is an abundance of evidence of its taming to be found on many Egyptian monuments. A large number of mummified cats has also been found.

The frescoes dating from this period most frequently depict a handsome cat sitting upright in the characteristic pose we know so well; obviously the Egyptian artists found this position particularly attractive from a plastic point of view, but the cat was also depicted in a number of other ways. One of the most ancient Egyptian funeral monuments, dedicated to King Hana of the XI Dynasty, which was discovered in the necropolis at Thebes, represents the Pharaoh accompanied by his cat Bouhaki. Other tombs of various dynasties from the XVI to the XX

A popular woodcut that shows the superstitious association of cats with witches.

include representations and monuments dedicated to the cat, which can also be seen on certain Bubatsis coins; the goddess Bast, an object of special veneration in Ancient Egypt, was represented in the religious iconography by the head of a cat.

From Ancient Egypt, which had made the cat a sacred animal, its domestication spread towards the Orient which, however, did not offer it the same welcome. The Persians, for example, did not treat the cat with the same reverence, believing it to be a propagator of disease.

The cat next spread to Europe, first to Greece and then to Rome, but it was not particularly widely known in the ancient Greco-Roman civilisations. Romans did, however, breed cats to keep down rats, ferrets and weasels.

It appears that the familiar domestic cat was not introduced into Northern Europe before the tenth century. Brehm refers to a body of laws from Wales (dating to Hywel Dha, a tenth-century legislator) in which the qualities peculiar to the domestic cat were listed, as well as the punishments to be meted out to those who ill-treated or killed a cat. Even the price of cats was laid down according to whether it was a killer of rats or not; if it was, the cat's value doubled.

The features which should be present in the cat at the moment of sale were also carefully fixed to avoid all possibility of deception. The compensation for having killed a cat was a ewe and its lamb, or the amount of wheat which would be needed to cover the space between the tip of the cat's tail and the end of its muzzle. These laws show how comparatively rare the cat must have been at this time and in what high esteem it was held.

A cat's life was not always so easy or free from danger. For the most part, during the entire Middle Ages popular ignorance and religious fanaticism held it to be a depraved animal, an untrustworthy and treacherous creature completely dedicated to evil, the friend of Satan and accomplice of witches. A cat declared to be a witch's 'familiar spirit' was often tortured with its mistress and ended at the stake in the same purifying fire. Even apart from this cruel fate, the cat was often tortured by fanatics

In changing light, the pupils in a cat's eyes are subject to greater variation than are those of any other feline. Left. In dim light. Centre. In normal light. Right. In strong light.

anxious to satisfy their desire for violence. It was customary, for example, to burn cats alive in midsummer bonfires.

Nowadays most of the prejudices about cats have disappeared, although a few people still retain some unfounded beliefs, such as the superstition that black cats possess evil powers.

Domestic cats

As mentioned earlier, it is probable that present day breeds of domestic cat stem from those first Nubian wild cats which the Egyptians succeeded in domesticating. Given the cat's characteristic propensity for following a free and vagabond life, particularly when in season or heat, we have obtained from this first feline species the remarkable variety of diverse breeds to be found today: a diversity of breeds due as much to its particular freedom in reproduction as to the external factors which tend to produce modifications in the species of animals generally.

The system of artificial selection developed by man, that of using a particular genus to breed specimens possessing unmistakable racial characteristics, tends to establish a number of well-defined breeds. It is a question of applying certain methods of reproduction to special breeds; but it must not be forgotten that these methods of reproduction, so widely used in dog-breeding, for example, are still at an experimental stage, and great difficulties have been encountered when carrying out such selections even on a strictly controlled genetic basis.

Nevertheless it is possible to determine breed differences in certain species of cat on the basis of definite and verifiable rules. First comes the distinction between two main sub-species: the *long-haired* cats, including the Persian (with its various offshoots) and the Angora; and the *short-haired* cats, comprising the Siamese, the different varieties of European, the Russian-American Blue, the Blue Cats, and the Nubian or Abyssinian.

If another, more scientific principle is used as a basis, and the length and breadth of the tail is taken into consideration, the feline species can be divided into three sub-species: *those possessing a normal tail*, to which belong the majority of cats including the Angora cats, the black cats of Gambia, the Blue breed and the European varieties; *those possessing a short tail*, which occur especially in Southeast Asia; and, finally, the tailless sub-species, which contains one solitary breed from the Isle of Man, the Manx cat.

It seems logical to deal first with the common European cat, which is the one most widespread in the Western world. Even though its appearance may not have made it so famous or admired as the cats of other, more elegant and aristocratic breeds, in the writer's opinion it is the one which contributes most to the picture of the domestic cat so dear to our imagination.

Common European cats are widespread all over the world, the best-known of them being the tabby cat. Two main types of tabby are recognised, the evidence, according to some scientists, of two separate lines of descent: the spotted and the striped tabbies.

Among the European varieties there are also some types of cat which have coats of only one colour without any markings. In such cases the only possible colours found are black, white, red and cream: the two latter are, however, very rare and difficult to rear. There are some cats with coats of three colours which are not greatly different from others of the same breed; different colour combinations occur and such cats are too numerous to list, but the best known is the tortoiseshell. One peculiarity, however, distinguishes these from all other cats: they are almost invariably female.

Persian cats

After briefly listing the characteristics of the common European cat, we come to that favourite of the elegant drawing room, the Persian cat. The Persian is a *de luxe* animal, to the extent that it does not display carnivorous instincts and is often slow and lazy. However, it is endowed with good intelligence which tends to make one

Left to right. Tail of European wild cat; tail of striped tabby; tail of Persian cat; tail of Siamese cat; tail of Siamese cat showing corkscrew twist.

forget its congenital defects. The fur, which can be of various colours, is formed of a great many very long fine hairs.

The Persian Chinchillas are one of the most recent varieties of this breed; they derive from the silver tabby, but, unlike the latter, are not striped. The fur tends to be clear in colour; breeding is very difficult; the eyes are green or dark blue.

The Cream Persians are also of comparatively recent origin. They are admired and much in demand because of the clear colour of their fur. Their eyes are orange.

The Red Persians, which can sometimes be spotted, are very rare and are almost extinct. Some breeders are still trying to raise them but the results are negative more often than not.

The Silver Persian in every way resembles the Persian Chinchilla as regards colour, while the markings recall those of the tabby cat. The eyes can be green or brown.

The Tortoiseshell Persians have a European equivalent, the European tortoiseshell. This Persian variety, which has a highly characteristic appearance, displays the same three colours which are present in the European cat. These Persians are always female.

Siamese cats

The Siamese breed is also much admired. It differs considerably from the others and its origins are still wrapped in mystery. All that is known is that the earliest specimens, imported into England at the end of the seventeenth century, came from the King of Siam's palace, and that he had lavished particular care on their breeding and selection. From these 'English' Siamese are descended all those to be found today.

The characteristics which distinguish them from all other cats would seem to arise from peculiarities beyond their considerably different physical appearance, and to be due to certain hereditary factors such as the period of ovulation and gestation in the females and the characteristic psychology of the males.

Siamese cats are very independent, although they can become so attached to their masters that they can sometimes display signs of jealousy. They are also hunters, but showing a marked preference for all winged creatures: they refuse utterly to hunt mice. Extremely responsive to affection, they like being taken for walks on a lead. However, at the risk of appearing contradictory, it must be admitted that they unquestionably retain a number of the characteristics displayed by wild cats; they do not like to be shut in and they prefer to live near green, open spaces.

Very similar to the Siamese, even to the point of leading specialists astray, are the Burmese cats. Their chief distinguishing characteristic is a dark brown colouring which becomes somewhat lighter on the chest and underparts. The Burman (Burmese 'Sacred' cat), on the other hand, has similar colouring to the Siamese but has much longer fur like the Persian. The head is more like the Persian's in structure; the eyes, like those of Siamese cats, are blue and almond shaped.

Blue cats

The Blue, a variety of the common European, is one of the breeds now most in demand. Tall and sturdy in stature, and an excellent mouser, it is brave, intelligent and a pleasant, affectionate companion in spite of its impressive size and shy nature.

The Russian-American Blue closely resembles the Blue, differing only in having a leaner, more elegant body and a smaller, more pointed, face. The eyes are green, not yellow, and its profile more elongated. The colour of the fur is almost identical in both species, though in the Russian-American variety it may possibly reflect a blue sheen.

Tailless cats

Finally, perhaps the strangest breed of all – the Manx cat, so-called because it originated on the Isle of Man. It has one very distinct characteristic: the almost complete absence of any tail. Another peculiarity of this breed is the greater development of its hind legs in comparison with the front, which gives it a rather strange gait, more like that of a rabbit than a feline. The fur can be of any colouring or marking.

Habits and character

Much has been recorded of the life and habits of the cat but, both in the distant past as well as more recently, it is generally a mere repetition of current beliefs and superficial statements. Although the cat's psychology and domestication has been studied much less profoundly than has that of the dog, the greatest measure of a cat's attraction lies precisely in its character and habits.

The cat's characteristics have often been compared, and actually set against those of its traditional rival, usually to the advantage of the dog, whose undisputed qualities have been extolled with scarcely objective praise. That false beliefs still prevail in this field, where everyone can verify and revise his opinions for himself, merely demonstrates that to err is human. We shall see to what extent these ill-conceived opinions can be substantiated.

In spite of these criticisms, the cat's admirers are enthusiasts sheltered from the prevailing scepticism; moreover, they are very numerous and their confidence never seems to be misplaced.

A cat's psychology is certainly more complex than that of a dog and therefore does not lend itself so well to precise classification, for example into traits pertaining to a special breed; what is possible to achieve to some extent with dogs, proves very difficult in the case of cats. Thus it is not possible to determine with sufficient accuracy common psychological characteristics for each breed of cat. Moreover, when considering the animal world, man is still too human in his attitudes, too subjective: he judges animals in terms of his own reactions and from this stem his continual mistakes in animal psychology.

Traditional literature presents the cat to us as the freest, most independent and most hostile to discipline of all domestic animals. It is precisely these qualities – or, according to some people, defects – that give a cat that particular charm mentioned earlier, a charm which is perhaps a little mysterious.

The cat's attitude towards man, many people think, is fickle. It almost seems as if the cat is never able to overcome some ancestral mistrust of the human race. Certainly, the wild cat is one of the animals most distrustful of man.

However, it must not be thought that the cat is entirely lacking in gratitude or that it is indifferent towards those who show love; the affection which the cat feels for its owner is constantly conditioned by the attitude of the owner. If it is treated with justice and kindness one can be sure that it will never betray its master's affection. But it must not be forgotten that the attachment felt by a cat is, by its nature, exclusive. It nearly always attaches itself to one person and not to all those with whom it is familiar. Its attachment is total to the extent of jealousy, which it does not hesitate to show when the occasion arises.

Reference has been made to the cat's friends and enemies. Buffon, one of the cat's fiercest detractors, describes it in these terms: 'The cat is a faithless domestic animal which is only kept in order to pit it against another, even more disagreeable domestic enemy that is difficult to catch . . .', and again, '. . . although these animals more often than not display a certain gracefulness when they are young, nevertheless they possess an innate malice, a falseness of character, which increases with time and experience. Born thieves, with good training cats become as smooth and deceitful as swindlers.'

Raiberti, another of the cat's detractors, wrote in his *Physiology of the Cat*: 'What an evil, deeply dissimulating animal, a vicious snarling creature which scratches you after a caress. It is unrivalled in its disobedience and obstinacy. An egoist, in truth, heedless of everything which does not touch upon its own interests, all its craftiness is for malice and perfidies of all kinds;

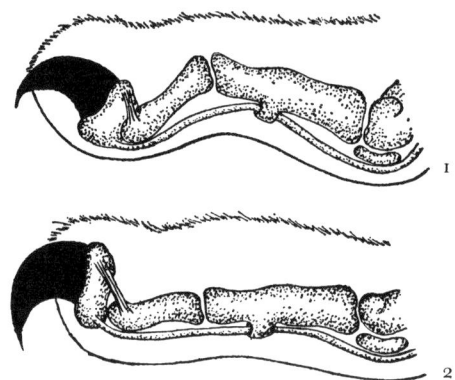

1) Cat's claw in retractile position.
2) Cat's claw at the ready.

obsequious like a sybarite; idle by profession; born thief and thief for the pleasure of stealing; cowardly when confronted by the strong, bloodthirsty and cruel towards the weak; for complete wickedness it lacks only the weapon of speech.'

For all that, the cat never lacks for friends or enthusiastic admirers, who have always loved it down through the ages. According to a Muslim legend, the Prophet Mahomet himself felt a particular affection for these creatures and this is demonstrated by this touching little story.

One day, while Mahomet was sitting meditating, his cat, Muezza, came and lay down on the capacious sleeve of his coat which was trailing on the ground beside him. Sitting immobile because of his inner contemplation, Mahomet did not stir and the cat fell asleep. The sun rose high in the sky and then sank towards the horizon. When his contemplation ended, and Mahomet wished to get up, he saw the cat asleep on his coat sleeve, looking the picture of bliss. Therefore, in order not to disturb Muezza's sleep, the prophet took a pair of scissors and cut off the sleeve of his coat.

In a text devoted to the habits and different breeds of cat, Faelli mentions many admirers of the feline tribe. The Roman general Scipio Nasica owned a tabby cat of which he was extremely fond. After Laura's death, Petrarch had no other companion to share his solitude, and the skeleton of the poet's cat is preserved in the Padua Museum. Le Tasse dedicated a sonnet to his little friend, begging it to give him the light of its eyes to illuminate his work at night. Leonardo da Vinci painted a picture of the Virgin and Child in which a cat can be seen playing with the infant Jesus. There were many more of whom Faelli only gives the names: Veronese, Grosley, Fontenelle, Gozzi, Montaigne, the astronomer Barode, who introduced the cat to the heavens by naming a constellation of stars after it; Richelieu, Colbert, Châteaubriand, who found lyrical phrases with which to praise the animal's grace, its independent character, its air of indifference and authority and the impression of sensuality which emanates from the attitudes it adopts; and Moncrieff, the historian, for whom the Académie Française opened its doors in honour of his *History of Cats*.

However, this formidable band of admirers, composed chiefly of artists and men of letters whose imaginations were fired by the character of the cat, its subtle, discreet and somewhat exotic charm, scarcely mention its intelligence in their panegryics. In point of fact, the intelligence of the cat is often underestimated. Nowadays there seems little doubt that the cat's intelligence is one of the most developed in the animal kingdom.

In the *Intelligence of Animals*, Romanes mentions many cases where cats have given proof of an acute intelligence and almost of the faculty of reason. Owners of domestic cats can surely produce frequent examples to support this claim. For example, Romanes tells how, when the servants used to attract a crowd of birds to the window by scattering breadcrumbs, the cat would get into the habit of waiting nearby for the more unwary or greedy birds. But during the summer months, this practice having ceased, the cat found itself deprived of its easy prey. It found its own answer to the problem. It collected up all the breadcrumbs it could find and scattered them to attract the birds.

Moreover, apart from intelligence, the cat possesses many appreciable qualities. Organically it is an almost perfect 'machine': its delicate senses are highly developed, notably its sense of hearing, touch and the sense of physical size; its sense of smell is not quite so acute but still more than good enough for normal use; its sight is keen, particularly by night.

In its dealings with man, a cat's behaviour can produce great surprises for anyone who troubles to train it with a certain amount of care. It has been amply demonstrated that the cat is perfectly capable of performing many of the activities for which other domestic animals are highly prized.

Notably in the country or in isolated places, where the cat has a chance to live in closer contact both with nature

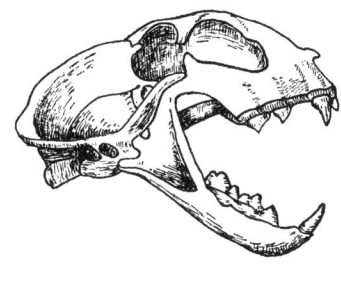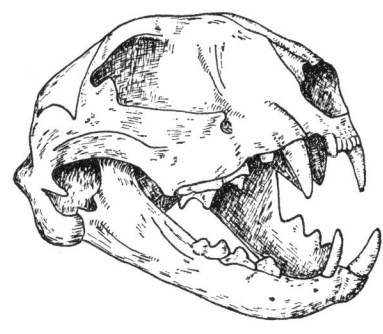

The skull of a lynx (far left) compared with the skull of a cat. A common characteristic of both felines is the flatness of the upper part of the skull, which is thus elongated: as a result, the antero-posterior diameter is noticeably greater than the vertical diameter.

and with its master, it can establish close bonds of co-operation and friendship, and show itself capable of quite remarkable feats of training. It is known that cats have been trained to guard, and miaow unceasingly when a stranger approaches the gate. Moreover, cats can show outstanding courage: one cat, when it thought its mistress to be in danger, attacked the aggressor without any consideration for his size or the risks involved.

There are innumerable examples of cats who, at the death of their masters, refused all nourishment and let themselves starve to death. Can there be any better proof that this 'egotist' has a sense of affection and faithfulness? But no cat can be expected to show either faithfulness, affection, or trust unless this is reciprocated by its owners.

Rearing your cat

Because of its feline and independent nature, the cat does not demand any special care unless it is intended to apply a rational breeding system, either in order to obtain racial differences or in order to improve a specific breed.

In that case it is absolutely necessary to follow certain basic rules: the areas set aside for this purpose should be furnished with benches, tables and wooden boxes; and there should be access to the outdoor world, to the garden or a balcony, where the cat can enjoy the fresh air and sunshine it needs for its health. To be really hygienic, its bedding should consist of paper or straw rather than cushions or covers which have the disadvantage of quickly becoming a home for parasites. The cat's sleeping basket must have sides high enough to keep out draughts.

These arrangements need not apply to cats kept in an apartment; moreover, animals that live in such places and do not have contact with their fellows adapt to their surroundings much more quickly. In their case it is only necessary to take some simple precautions: avoid, for example, exposing the animal to too damp an atmosphere, which would be detrimental to its health; see that its bed is put in a fairly warm place; although cats can live in quite a cold climate, a prolonged stay in a cold place, particularly at night, will certainly prove harmful in the long run.

Turning to food, do not forget that in its natural state the cat is essentially a carnivore. When domesticated, meat should therefore still be its main food; but not its only one, for its body also needs foods that are less rich in proteins such as milk, bread, cheese, cooked vegetables, with the occasional addition of fish and calves' liver.

Finally, remember that pork, salted or smoked, can cause painful inflammation and that your cat may well find left-over table scraps bad for its health. Sensible feeding is vital to a pet's well-being.

Cats are not subject to many diseases for they are fundamentally healthy animals. Apart from bronchitis and pneumonia, which can attack cats just as easily as man, there are rabies – only, however, if the cat is bitten by another infected animal – and canker of the ear, rare in well-fed specimens but a frequent complaint in strays. This can, however, be cured easily.

Thus it is clear that a cat does not present any danger to its master from the point of view of health; it cannot communicate any disease to him and, if a scratch from its claws should become infected, it is not the cat's fault alone, but also due to the fact that the necessary disinfectant has not been applied.

Distribution of the principal members of the cat family

European cats	Wild	European Wild Cat Northern Lynx
	Domestic	Common European Cat Blue Cat Russian-American Blue Cat Manx Cat
Asiatic cats	Wild	Pallas's Cat Fishing Cat Ocelot Jungle Cat Bengal Tiger Leopard Snow Leopard Clouded Leopard Indian Lion Temminck's Golden Cat Marbled Cat Flat-headed Cat
	Domestic	Siamese Cat Burmese Cat Chinese Cat Persian Cat Burman Cat
American cats	Wild	American Tiger Cat Margay Pampas Cat Northern Lynx Bobcat Ocelot Geoffroy's Cat Mountain Cat Jaguarondi Jaguar Kodkod Puma
	Domestic	Imported breeds
African cats	Wild	African Golden Cat African Wild Cat Jungle Cat Black-footed Cat Serval Cheetah Sand Cat Leopard Lion Lynx
	Domestic	Abyssinian Cat

Principal breeds of domestic cat

	SHORT-HAIRED CATS		LONG-HAIRED CATS
British	White (Blue Eyes, Orange Eyes, Odd Eyes) Black Blue British Cream Silver Tabby Red Tabby Brown Tabby Tortoiseshell Tortoiseshell-and-White Blue-Cream Bi-coloured Spotted Manx	**Persian**	Black White (Blue Eyes, Orange Eyes, Odd Eyes) Blue Red Cream Brown Tabby Silver Tabby Red Tabby Blue-Cream Bi-coloured Tortoiseshell Tortoiseshell-and-White Chinchilla Smoke
Foreign	Siamese Seal-Pointed Siamese Blue-Pointed Siamese Chocolate-Pointed Siamese Lilac-Pointed Siamese Tabby-Pointed Siamese Red-Pointed Siamese Tortie-Pointed Abyssinian Red Abyssinian Russian Blue Burmese Blue Burmese Brown Burmese Cream Burmese Blue-Cream Havana Cornish Rex Devon Rex	**Other Long-hairs**	Colourpoint Birman Turkish

1 Red-and-white fluffy kittens with some tabby markings, not pure pedigree. Kittens of any breed win us over by their disarming appeal and a touch of inherent savagery; these are the main ingredients of their fascination.

2 Cream long-hair cat of great beauty and considerable value. Popularly known as a Persian, it is distinguished by its long, silky hair and the round and broad head, full cheeks and broad muzzle.

3 According to the amount of light present, the pupil of the cat can contract or dilate, and in this way allows light to reach the particularly sensitive retina to afford a clear vision, irrespective of the quality and quantity of the surrounding light.

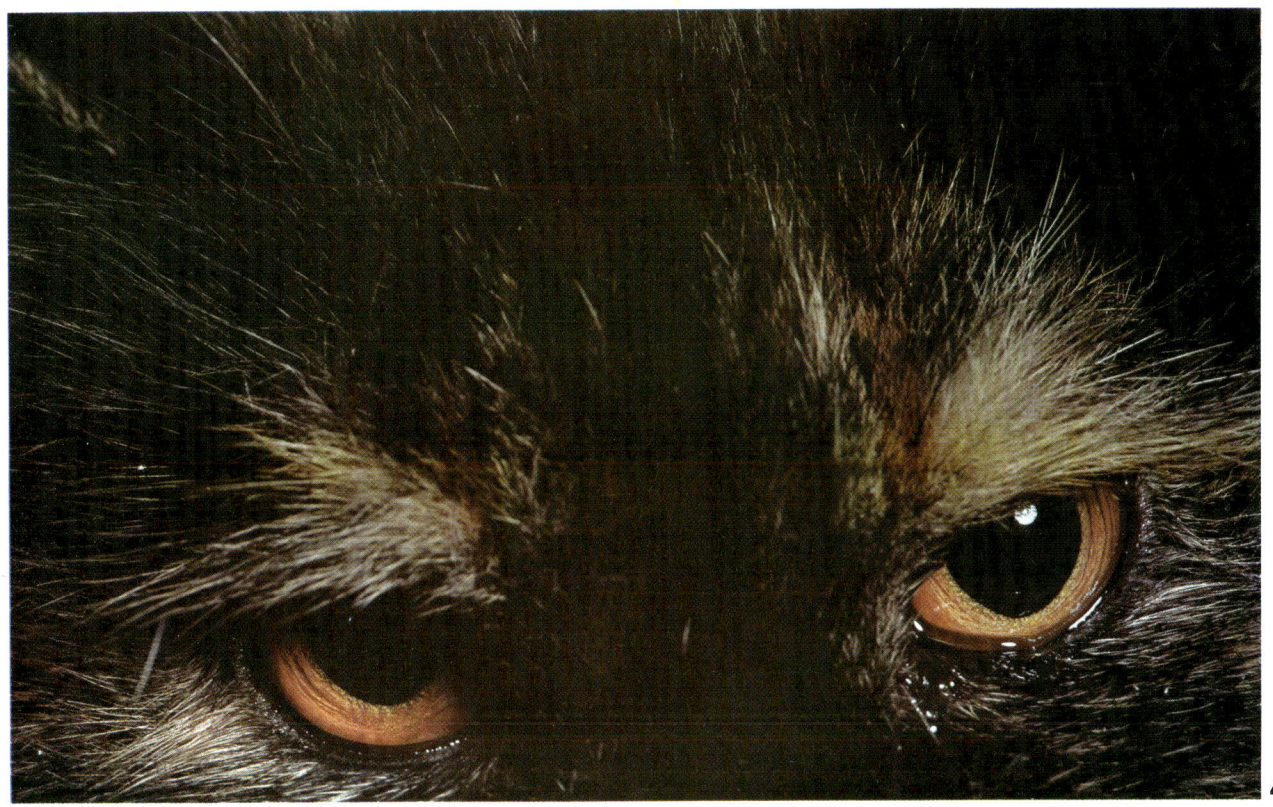

4-5 The eyes of the cat, as with all felines, have developed through natural evolution to allow clear and precise vision whether by night or day. The feeding requirements of this group of animals oblige them to hunt continually, which is more easily accomplished by night. Their pupils therefore are not round, as with many other animals, such as dogs and man. A cat's pupil forms a vertical slit which can dilate until it occupies the greater part of the eye, changing from an elliptical to a roundish form.

6 Red Tabby long-hair kittens   **7** Long-hair kittens   **8** Tabby-and-white kittens

When choosing a kitten make sure that the one you select is in perfect condition. Check that the kitten's eyes are bright and alert; its ears should be clean, its tongue pink, its nose soft and moist. The fur should be glossy and smooth and the skin free from any signs of sores and scabs. If you wish to breed or exhibit your cat, you will do best to go to a well-known or recommended breeder. Along with the kitten you will receive a pedigree, but remember that for a pedigree cat you will have to pay much more. If you want a cat merely as a pet and are not too particular about its background, go to a good pet shop. Take your kitten home in a comfortable box or basket, and give it a good deal of love and attention during the first week. It must get used to its new home and new faces and will sleep a lot of the time. At first it may feel lonely and even insist on sleeping on your bed, in which case you should give way. When it has settled down it will probably be content to sleep in a warm, comfortable, draught-free box or basket.

7

8

9 Milk is certainly the basic food of kittens, but even when mature, and eating a richer and more varied diet, cats still need this form of liquid nourishment, because it both quenches the thirst and provides excellent nourishment.

10 Brown Tabby short-hair quins.   **11** Cream long-hair twins.   **12** A litter of short-hair kittens
Kittens are by nature mischievous and playful, and while perfectly capable of finding things to amuse themselves and one another, they do like to be played with or have their own 'toys'. The simplest things can offer them hours of amusement – ping-pong balls, cotton reels, screwed-up balls of paper, pieces of string – in fact anything which they can roll or pounce upon. One personal toy which can be bought for a small amount of money is a catnip mouse. This offers a wonderful smell for a kitten, which will become most attached to it and often play with it.

11

12

13 Tabby-and-white kitten. It will make a lovable pet but is unlikely to win an award at a cat show because its colouring does not conform to the breed standard. Most kittens are born with their eyes closed and are unable to walk, but they soon develop and quickly display their instinctive urge to hunt mice, crickets, lizards and ants. They do not hesitate even when young to climb into the branches of a tree in the hope of catching an unwary bird.

14 Silver Tabby short-hair male kitten of 6 months, with perhaps a little too much white on its chin to make it a champion. Tabby markings should be clearly defined and not at all blurred. Like all British short-hair cats the Silver Tabby should have a powerful body, a broad head with well-developed cheeks and fur that is short, fine and close.

15 The cat's teeth present all the particular characteristics of the carnivorous feline. The dental pattern is as follows: three upper and lower incisors, two upper and lower canines, three upper and two lower premolars, eight upper and seven lower molars, making a total of 30 teeth. The kittens are born without teeth, and by about two months have a complete set of milk teeth, which will subsequently be replaced by second adult teeth. The cat's molars like those of all felines have a very serrated surface.

16 Tabby-and-white short-hair kittens, the obvious result of cross-breeding. These little cats do not seem to be too worried by their lack of pedigree – a skein of green wool presents quite enough difficulties.

17 Black and white cat. Like every other feline, the domestic cat possesses a remarkable sense of balance, which allows it to venture on to window ledges, balconies, posts, branches and narrow gutters, without any sense of danger and more important still, without the slightest trace of vertigo. In the very rare cases where a cat falls from its perch, it is never the result of its own imprudence, but is always due to some external cause; its perfect muscular co-ordination allows it to fall so that it hits the ground with all four paws ready for the impact.

16

17

18

19

20

18 Meat is the cat's main food, but it is wrong to think that simply by offering it the same amount daily you assure its good health and nourishment. The quality of the meat is of extreme importance in the rearing of cats; contrary to popular belief, lights, spleen and tripe are not suitable for the cat, although it finds them tasty. These foods give too little nourishment in comparison to their size, and distend the cat's stomach. Meat and fish are the cat's staple food and no matter how fastidious your cat may be, it will rarely refuse fish or meat altogether. It will probably enjoy raw or cooked meat, and beef, lamb, rabbit and chicken are acceptable. Rabbit and chicken should be given sparingly and should be carefully boned. Liver can be given as a treat. Fish should always be cooked and all the bones removed.

19 Even after weaning, when kittens are able to feed themselves, milk is still an essential part of a cat's diet, and remains so throughout its life. As well as milk the cat needs meat for the protein it contains, small amounts of cooked vegetables for their mineral salts, and finally raw yolk and white of egg, which is also a valuable source of protein. Too much carbohydrate, from eating bread, cereals and starchy vegetables, is harmful to the cat's essentially carnivorous digestive system, and can provoke intestinal disorders and scabs on the skin.

21   22

20 White British short-hair cat with blue eyes. The combination of a perfectly white coat and blue eyes is particularly prized by breeders in spite of the fact that most of these cats are congenitally deaf. The breed can also have orange eyes or odd eyes (one blue and one yellow). The rearing and care of white cats with blue eyes presents many difficulties, for as about 75 per cent are born deaf there is the problem of communication between cat and owner.

21 Red-and-white short-hair kitten, whose white chin and paws prevent it from being an outstanding specimen of tabby markings. The tabby cat is the most common European cat; in Britain three varieties of short-hair are recognised – the Brown Tabby, the Silver and the Red. The markings should stand out distinctly from the background coat colouring. This one has the deep copper colour eyes which are a striking feature of the Red Tabby.

22 Here is another kitten whose sense of adventure has induced him to climb on to the top of a post, without a thought of how he is going to get down again. In fact it quite frequently happens that young cats like this climb up into some dangerous spot, do not know how to get down again, and miaow piteously for help.

23

23 Brown Tabby short-hair kittens. They make ideal companions and although they are not considered to be particularly valuable, they are frequently preferred to more prized but less sympathetic breeds.

24 Chinchilla. The eyes of the Persian Chinchilla present a singular appearance; it is the only one of the long-hair cats that has black-rimmed eyes. Beautiful though this cat undoubtedly is, its ears are slightly too big and its eyes should be emerald or sea green.

25 Brown Tabby short-hair. Note the white chin, a fault which occurs in many Tabbies and is exceedingly difficult to breed out. The Tabby is perhaps the most well-known of all domestic cats. The markings should be clearly and uniformly defined. The colour of the fur can be red (Red Tabby) formed by reddish rings on a fawn basic colour, or brown (Brown Tabby) with brown rings on a reddish basic colour, or silver (Silver Tabby) with dark blue markings on a light grey basic colour.

24

25

26 Black and white cat with kittens. Many cat lovers think that of all the many different varieties of the domestic cat the black and white cat is the most intelligent, and they do in fact show a great capacity for astutely evaluating and solving unexpected problems. They are particularly handsome, with their long white whiskers and black faces.

27 Red Tabby short-hair, but not a good example of the breed as the coat contains too much white. In Britain the standard for the breeds is laid down by breed societies and the Governing Council of the Cat Fancy, and breeders strive to achieve the perfection which is contained in these published standards. Many cats of good pedigree, such as this one, fail to achieve high honours in the show world but make excellent pets.

28

29

28 Tri-colour cats have a mottled coat with black, white and red markings in fairly equal proportions. Cats with a leg or breast of one colour are not very highly prized. The cat shown here is a typical example of a predominantly white tri-colour. They are very common in France, particularly in the region bordering on Spain near Perpignan and the Pyrenees. This is the reason why it is sometimes known there as-the Spanish cat.

29 Although the cat is a very clean animal, kittens, like puppies, are prey to all sorts of infections and special care must be taken during their rearing. The infection they catch most readily is called feline infectious enteritis. The symptoms are varied, and can range from outbreaks of sores to dysentery and pneumonia. All kittens should be taken to the vet for inoculations against this dangerous disease.

30 Tabby with a mixed litter. The gestation period in cats is about 60 days and ends with a litter of 4 to 8 kittens who are born at intervals of about 10 to 20 minutes. The mother generally tries to hide herself away in a dark place to give birth, and this instinctive behaviour should be fostered by the owner, who should prepare some clean and suitable spot away from the house. After the birth of each kitten the mother bites the cord and eats the placenta. It would be quite wrong to try and prevent her doing this for misplaced reasons of hygiene. Nature in fact intends her to do so, because the placenta contains substances which stimulate the milk supply.

30

31

32

33

31 This long-haired cat with her kittens is a cross-bred with almost Tortoiseshell-and-White colouring – but the colour should be deeper. The kittens too are cross-bred; their exact colouring cannot be stated with accuracy as it is likely to change as they grow older.

32 A Brown Tabby long-hair with some white markings which make it more of a pet than a show cat. A cat, while having no prehensile fingers, shows much versatility when it comes to holding, shaking and gripping. It can either use its claws, or keep them retracted to avoid damaging delicate objects.

33 Red Tabby short-hair with rather indefinite markings. With this variety the colour must be a deep rich red and not sandy or ginger.

34 When it comes to finding a comfortable spot for a nap, the cat usually makes an excellent choice. It loves dry sunny places, chooses the softest cushion, the greenest grass and if it can find an empty deck chair, that suits it even better.

35 Although Tabbies are not as highly prized as Persians and Siamese, they do produce some very splendid examples quite capable of holding their own at cat shows.

36 The apparent laziness of the cat should not be confused with passivity or indifference. It is ready to spring to attention should the need arise.

37–41 The love and the care that the mother lavishes on her kittens is evidence of the 'parental nurture' that every animal gives its young. The mother cares for her kittens very conscientiously while she is still feeding them, but once they are weaned she feels less closely bound by them, and if her kittens are then taken away, she recovers quite quickly. The kitten should be breast-fed for about 40 days after birth; it is then possible for it to be weaned as it is old enough to feed itself. One cannot stress too highly the importance of the mother's milk for the health of the kitten, but there are cases where the mother, for physiological reasons, has been unable to feed her young. If this happens it is necessary to feed the kitten artificially by means of a bottle. Cow's milk is not advised as it is much less nutritious than cat's milk, and not sufficient for the kitten's growth. A specially prepared artificial milk containing all the necessary ingredients can be used, or failing that pasteurised milk to which has been added the yolk of an egg. It is also necessary to remember that the young kitten is sometimes too weak to be able to suck directly from a bottle, but it is possible to feed it by squeezing milk directly into the mouth by means of a medicine dropper. This is a very time-consuming business, but the necessary patience will be well rewarded, since the cat when adult will be just as strong, healthy and lively as a breast-fed cat.

42 To carry her young from place to place, the mother delicately picks up the kitten by taking the loose scruff of its neck between her teeth. It is possible for us to pick a kitten up by the scruff of the neck without endangering any part of its delicate body, which would be likely to happen if it were squeezed round the stomach, or if it were picked up by the front paws.

43

44

45

43 Cats are interested in their surroundings, and always explore their territory very thoroughly, aided by their sense of smell.

44–8 As you can see in this series of photographs, when a cat really wants to reach something, it usually succeeds. Its natural ability allows it to climb, jump up and keep its balance in all sorts of positions, and its intelligence tells it the best way to go about the matter. A clumsy cat, like an unfaithful dog, is difficult to imagine.

46

47

48

49 In spite of the traditional hostility which is supposed to exist between cats and dogs, the two animals in the photograph seem to be the best of friends. Such an occurrence is by no means unusual, particularly when the two animals have been reared in the same household.

50 Cream long-hair kitten. This breed has proved difficult to produce to the required standard, and good specimens are the result of painstaking selective breeding and care.

51 Chocolate-pointed Siamese cat. Introduced into Europe from Bangkok, in the late nineteenth century, the Siamese cat very quickly became famous in the Western world for its proud but sweet nature, and its physical beauty. Today they are bred in many countries and several handsome new varieties have appeared.

52 Red-pointed Siamese. This is a more recent breed introduced by an English breeder as a result of particularly careful selection. The name is suggested by the reddish-gold shade of the fur localised on the points where on the Chocolate-pointed Siamese it would be dark brown.

53 Chocolate-pointed Siamese cat and kittens. One of the many differences between European and Siamese cats is the gestation period: in the Siamese this lasts three or four days longer. It also has fewer ovarian cycles and is on heat less often.

54 Kittens of the Blue-pointed Siamese. The Blue-pointed Siamese differs from the Chocolate-pointed Siamese because its mask, tail and paws are grey-blue and not dark brown. In kittens this coloration is less distinct, because their colour tends to be uniform at birth; the ones shown in the photograph, however, are clearly different from their brown cousins.

55 Lilac-pointed Siamese. This colouring, which is much appreciated, is very difficult to obtain. The result of crossing Blue-pointed Siamese, the Lilac-pointed Siamese – the lilac being on the mask, ears, paws and tail – has one other singularity which distinguishes it from the Chocolate-pointed Siamese: the length of the mask is much more pronounced.

56 Although it has a proud and independent nature, the Siamese cat loves man's company and responds to his affection by forming a jealous and exclusive attachment to him; it becomes deeply unhappy if it feels betrayed or if its owner shows interest in any other animal, particularly another cat.

57 With all Siamese cats, breeders have long been divided on the subject of the tail. Judges have still not agreed whether to accept or reject the short-tailed variety, but in the case of a Siamese who scores highly on all other points they will usually overlook this condition.

58

59

42

58 The temperament of the Siamese cat is different from that of the Tabby. They still retain a touch of wildness which years of domestication has not extinguished. It is not difficult to rear a Siamese kitten, but it is necessary to remember that they need lots of space, meticulous hygiene and a great deal of affection from their owner.

59 Brown Burmese cats which would lose points when on show, for the eye colour is too green. In the Brown Burmese the eyes should be yellow chartreuse, and yellowish green in the Blue variety. Burmese cats are obviously closely linked to the Siamese. Breeders differ on how the breed originated: whether it is a variation of the Siamese or vice-versa. They have been fairly common in North America for 40 years. The first pair to be seen in Britain arrived from the United States in 1947, and the breed was officially recognised in 1952.

60-1 Birman long-hairs, descendants of the sacred cats that were the guardians of the temples in Burma. Although the coat is the same dark colour as the Siamese, with ears, mask, tail and paws dark brown and the rest of the body rather light in colour, the Birman must really be considered as a breed of its own. Its appearance gives an impression of robustness, despite the slender body; the paws are short, the head is rounded, and the muzzle large and blunt. The eyes are marvellously expressive, deep and blue. Other characteristics of this type of cat are the large bushy tail and the dark paws gloved with white. It is a blend of Siamese and Persian, but not sacrificing the individual qualities of either.

64

62–3 Long-haired Colourpoint. The beauty of this cat hardly needs elaboration. It is a much sought breed, but their health is delicate due to difficulty in adjusting to poor climates. This is a handicap which can easily be overcome if the owner takes care. It is very popular in the United States and Canada, where it is known as the Himalayan.

64 This cross-bred long-hair is predominantly Chinchilla, with the markings of that breed clearly showing in the nose tip of brick-red and the blue-green eyes. There is a mistaken belief in some quarters that long-hairs (or Persians as they are popularly called) are consumed with vanity – but this is a gross injustice. Although they love attention, they are affectionate towards their owners and always respond to them.

65 Tortoiseshell Persian. The face of the Persian cat is very different from that of other cats. The mask is much larger, the nose is flatter, and the ears are slightly shorter and wider at the base.

66 We have already mentioned when describing the European tortoiseshell cat, the origin of the distinctive colouring, and we also underlined the fact that this holds true for the Persian. In the photograph you can see the tortoiseshell kitten beside its completely cream mother.

67 Shaded Silver long-hair cat with kittens; this breed is not recognised in Britain. The best specimens have green eyes, and so the mother and her litter would lose marks on this account on the show bench.

68 A cross-bred long-hair cat that is probably the result of the mating of a Smoke with a Silver Tabby.

69 Cats do not very often suffer from mouth infections, because their saliva has a strong disinfectant action. However if the cat eats something too strong or too hot the mouth can be scalded, and this is very painful. The treatment must be precise and a vet must be consulted.

70

70 A fine specimen of a Shaded Silver long-hair, a breed that still awaits recognition in Britain. The coat texture is important in judging long-hairs; it must be silky and not at all harsh or woolly.

71 No printing process can do justice to the beauty of the Blue-Cream long-hair cat. This is a difficult variety to breed because the colour of the coat must be an exact mixture of blue and cream; cats with extended areas of one or other colour should be avoided for competition purposes. The small number of males is another characteristic of this variety.

72 Cats are very playful young animals. It is probably this which makes them such attractive pets.

71

72

73 Although these kittens are so different in appearance they are in fact brothers, and both of them are pedigree. This is easily explained by a fundamental genetic law: if you cross two subjects of pure race but of a different colour (for example a Blue and a Cream Persian) the resultant young will all be hybrid; if in turn two of these hybrids are mated, half the litter will be more hybrids, one quarter pure-bred of the one type, the other quarter pure-bred of the other type.

74 A beautiful Chinchilla long-hair which would be even nearer the perfection laid down in the standard for the breed if its eyes were a deeper green.

75 Black Persian. This variety is very difficult to produce, and perfectly black ones with copper-coloured eyes are the most rare and sought-after of all. Good results can be obtained in second-generation cats by crossing Blue Persians with Black Persians. Again it is difficult to tell by looking at the kittens which will be the perfect specimens when full grown: you can carefully rear a whole litter only to find that you do not have a single champion. In order to keep the coat in good condition it is necessary to pay close daily attention to it. It is important not to let the cat sit for too long in the sun, or the fur will take on a reddish aspect; the fur itself must be combed and brushed frequently.

76 Orange-eyed White Persian cat. The White Persian, like the Black Persian is very delicate. Brushing and combing the fur is essential, and the whiteness of it can be enhanced by using a special white powder. The fur itself must be absolutely white, the tail thick and bushy, the eyes large and round. The orange-eyed variety is comparatively recent, and just as popular as the traditional blue-eyed variety.

77 Smoke Persian. These are a comparatively rare type of Persian with black or dark blue surface fur and a white undercoat. They are not a pure strain and can only be obtained by cross-breeding.

78 A cross-bred long-hair, probably the result of mating a Chinchilla with a Cream. This particular colouring is neither much sought after nor very valuable, but the cross-breeding has produced a very attractive cat.

79 Two Shaded Silver cats, a breed very popular on the Continent though not in Britain.

78

79

80 The sculptural and dignified bearing of Persian cats is proverbial.

81 Cream Persian with orange eyes. In order to be judged a perfect specimen and be awarded maximum points, the coat of a Cream Persian must be one colour only, without the slightest marking, and of a pale shade – the darker colours much in vogue a few years ago are no longer acceptable. The fur should be long, silky and lustrous; the eyes must be orange and should be very large and limpid.

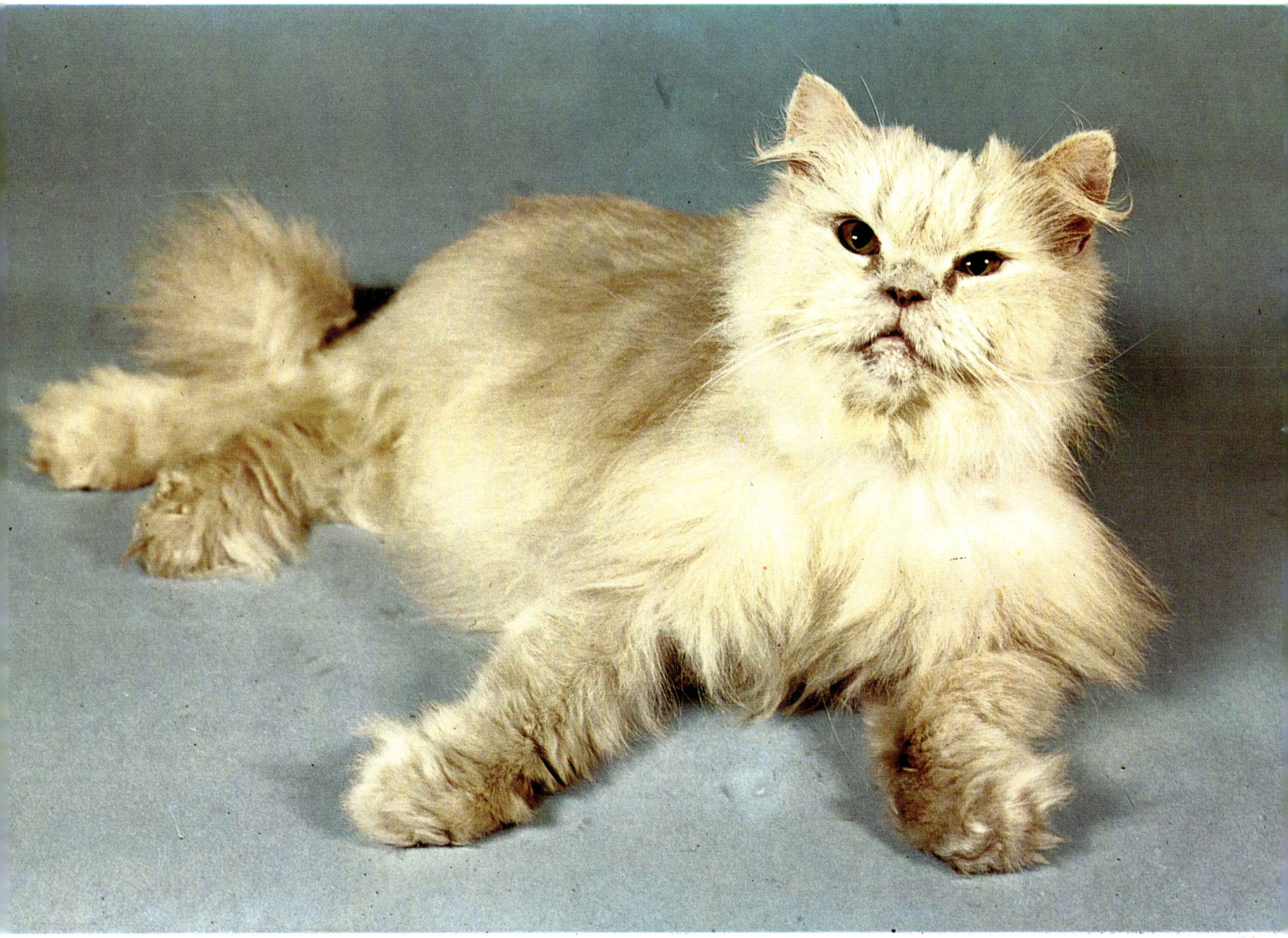

82 Cream Persian. All possible shades of cream from ivory to yellow and fawn are allowed for this particular type, as long as the strength of the colour does not exceed certain limits set down by breeder's clubs. Apart from too deep a colour, it is not allowed to have a white tuft on the tail, but a cream tuft on the ears is highly regarded.

83 Like all four-legged animals, the cat finds it difficult to balance on its hind legs. The centre of gravity for a quadruped falls inside the area between its four paws. This means that if you prop the animal up on its hind legs, the centre of gravity falls outside the area occupied by the body, and it only retains its balance with considerable muscular effort.

84 Tortoiseshell Persian. For both the colour of their coats and their beautiful appearance, the Tortoiseshell Persian is one of the most popular varieties with both breeders and pet lovers. One of the very attractive features of these cats is the exceptional colour of their fur.

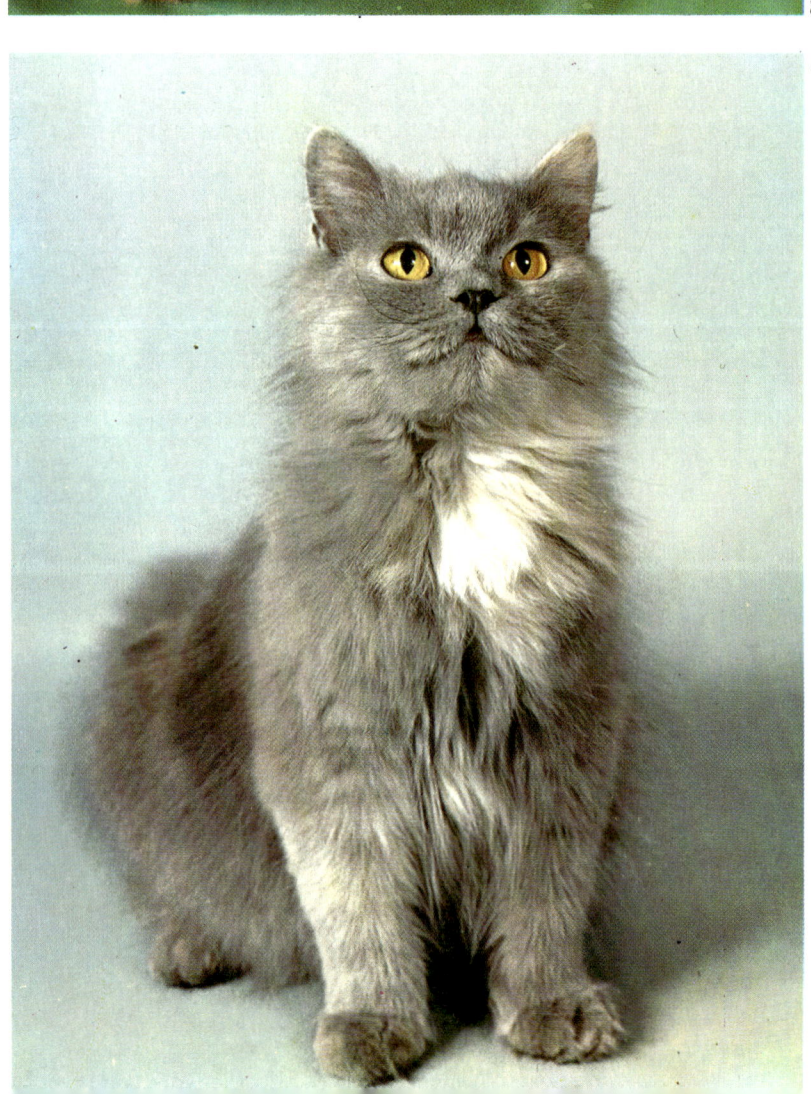

85 A Red Tabby long-hair kitten which might have had a champion's career in front of it if there had not been so much white in its coat.

86 This cat has a very distinctive white patch on its front, in contrast with the rest of the coat, which is the typical Blue Persian colour. This irregularity of colouring means that the cat, the result of careless breeding, will be excluded from cat shows in spite of its obvious beauty.

87 Cream, black, and reddish orange are the colours which make up the Tortoiseshell's coat. A perfect specimen of this type of colouring must have a harmonious blending of the component colours, with no single colour predominating over the other two. A very valuable variety of the Tortoiseshell Persian is one in whose coat the three basic colours are intermingled with white streaks. This variety is, however, very rare.

88 Blue Persian. Although they first made their appearance in Europe at a rather late date – towards the end of the nineteenth century – these magnificent and attractive cats, with their gentle and friendly disposition, had already been established as a breed for several centuries in Persia. A light coloured coat is most highly thought of nowadays, but extreme care is needed, for the selective breeding which results in the light blue shade may weaken the stock. This makes the rearing of this type of Persian extremely difficult and costly.

89 During the first few days of feeding, the mammary glands of the cat do not produce real milk, but a thick yellowish substance called colostrum which is rich in mineral salts and has a low fat content. It is very nourishing for the kitten, provides immunity and has laxative properties, all indispensable in adapting it to the rigours of life.

88

89

90 The appearance of cats on postage stamps is an indication of their widespread appeal. This is a set issued by Poland.

91 People who are not fond of Persian cats usually attack their character. They claim it is lazy, sly, faithless, unintelligent and vain. No doubt some Persians do have these faults, but it seems excessive to attribute so many bad qualities to all the individuals of one breed.

92 Russian Blue short-hair pregnant queen. This is a well-known breed in Europe and North America. Its characteristics are: short, glossy, grey-blue coat, triangular head, lit up by slanting, emerald green eyes, an agile, slim body, and a long, slender tail.

93 Abyssinian cat. This is the cat that most reminds us of the Egyptian cat of antiquity, or rather of the votive statues of them which have survived. Its fur is short, smooth, and of a uniform golden colour. However on closer examination each hair is seen to be made up of several colours: a golden area, a lighter one, and a brown one. The body is slender, ending in a long tail, and the head is triangular with large round eyes, although this specimen has a little too much white around the mouth, and its head is too round for perfection.

92

93

94

95

96

94 As well as its dental formation, which is characteristic of all felines, the cat's tongue is particularly adapted to the hunter's life: in order to facilitate ingestion of water or food, the tongue can roll into an arched shape very easily, and the rough spines which cover the surface make an excellent brush for tangled fur.

95 Persian Chinchilla. The eyes of a Persian are very different from those of a Tabby, or a Siamese. They are larger and rounder. Slanting eyes, which are required in the Siamese and tolerated in the Tabby, are never allowed in the case of the Persian; they must also be perfectly open. The colour can vary from orange to copper, from intense blue to green, but it must always be pure. A veining or a touch of another colour can eliminate a cat, perfect in all other respects, from a contest.

96 Abyssinian kitten with far too much white in its coat to make it a show winner. Although it does not like to live in an apartment without a garden, where it can give full rein to its love of adventure, the Abyssinian cat has a gentle and affectionate nature which makes it an ideal companion, although it is rather independent.

97 Mosaic from Pompeii. Although the Romans were well aware of the cat, particularly in the last period of their civilisation, they did not consider it to be 'the friend of man' but rather a charming semi-wild animal. It was not generally allowed in the house and was only used to catch mice. Its beauty and gracious appearance inspired a number of mosaics, where it is usually shown attacking or devouring its prey.

98 Geoffroy's cat, *Felis geoffroyi*. This is a cat of medium size, found in the jungles of South America and particularly in the Amazon region. It prefers to hunt on rock ground where its speed and agility make it feel perfectly at home. Its coat is grey, flecked with black irregular spots, and the fur itself is thick but short. Geoffroy's cat, known in its own region by the curious name of *mbaracaya*, is considered to be closely related to the domesticated cat.

99 Caracal. The caracal is very similar to the Iynx, the only difference being the slightly smaller size and a generally more graceful and slender appearance. An excellent hunter, it relies on its remarkable speed to capture its prey, which are usually animals equally noted for their speed, such as antelopes and gazelles.

100 Bobcat or Bay Lynx, *Lynx rufus*. The bobcat is smaller than the ordinary lynx and cannot match the speed of most other wild cats. As a result it rarely attacks larger animals than itself unless driven by extreme hunger. It prefers hares, rabbits and rodents which it can pounce upon from strategic positions in trees. The characteristics peculiar to the bobcat are its short tail and small tufts on the ears. It can be found throughout most of North America.

101 Tiger, *Panthera tigris*. The tiger is the largest of the 'big cats' and can now only be found in Asia where its prey consists mainly of antelope, deer and wild pig. The mating season is very short and tigers will often fight to the death for possession of a female. A tigress can have up to six cubs although only an average of two are likely to survive into adulthood.

102 Serval. The serval is a wild cat found all over Africa south of the Sahara Desert. It has rather a gentle nature and it is one of the few wild cats that are easy to tame. Its appearance is also very different from that of other wild cats; it is larger, and its coat is more like that of a leopard. Its basic colour can vary greatly from a pale fawn to a reddish tone, with black spots or stripes distributed all over the body.